This Journal was born from a place of gratitude.

Gratitude to those who have invested in me physically, emotionally and spiritually over the years. To those who have seen me at my lowest and loved me back to life. To those who have believed in me and my dreams and championed me along the journey. To those who have called me higher. To those who have spoken truth to my heart, when all I could hear was lies. To those who made me feel seen, heard and known.

But most of all, to the one who has sat with me in the darkness, loving me without judgement. The one who selflessly took my sin, guilt and shame and smothered it in unconditional love. The one who has heard every cry and caught every tear. The one who showed me how to love myself again. My Jesus, my Saviour.

If you are here, you are most likely familiar with the feeling of not being enough. A feeling that leaves you wondering why you even bothered. A thought that constantly creeps in when you are just about to step out and try something new.

Well Enough is Enough!

Now is the time for you to realise your worth and move past the things that have been holding you back.
This Journal is a tool to help you work through some of the blocks that keep sending you around in circles and stop you from stepping out into the fullness of who you were created to be.

As you work through the journalling questions in this book, come with an open heart and follow the process. This is not a 'one - time fixes all' kind of thing (sorry to disappoint you!) It is a lifestyle change and a choice to work through the lies as they come up.

It starts with a declaration that 'Enough is Enough!' and ends with the knowledge that being *Enough IS Enough.*

Hello lovely one,

Do you know how special you are?

You are worthy of love and connection. Not because of anything that you do or say but because you were created with a unique purpose. You were fearfully and wonderfully made by your heavenly father, knit together in your mother's womb. You my darling are chosen and wanted.

You hold dreams within you that have long been buried and it's time to allow them to bubble to the surface. You have the strength and the courage that you need inside of you, they were placed there for this very moment. You are not alone on this journey.

You are beautiful, you carry hope to those around you. As you draw closer to Jesus, you light a path for others to do the same. You are a fiery trailblazer and this world needs you to leave your mark. Your giftings are not insignificant, they were placed within you for a reason. Feel the freedom to step out of the skin of who you think you 'should' be and put on the garments of who you were created to be.

Now is your time to shine. To be a beacon of light in the darkness. It's time to leave fear, shame and self-doubt at the foot of the cross and walk in the fullness that was intended for you. You are loved beyond measure, precious one. That knowledge is your superpower.

Stand firm on truth and know that You are **ENOUGH**.

With Love
Beki xx

Journalling 'How to'

You may have stacks of filled journals or you may have stacks of empty ones, we all love stationary right?! Whether this is your first time or something you do regularly, I thought a simple Journalling 'How to' may be helpful before we dive in.

•Create a space away from distractions. Make a drink, get comfy, and grab a pen! You might like some gentle background music and have your bible nearby.

•Two-way journalling is an open communication between us and God. We write down our thoughts and also allow space for God to talk back to us through our writing. There is space in this journal for both one or two-way journalling (and extra pages in the back if you need!)

•Take a moment to invite Holy Spirit and to give thanks that he wants to speak into your life today.

•Write. Don't overthink it. Just write.

•Then once you have finished the journalling session, read it back and highlight anything that may have come up for you.

This is in no way prescriptive; we are all unique so find what works for you. This is just ONE way. I love to set aside specific time, but I've also had some of my best journalling sessions in the car with a sleeping child in the back!

Ditching the lies

I lived for many, many years carrying the weight of expectation, both from others and from myself. I constantly strived for perfection and beat myself up about all the little things, as well as the big. I bought into the lie that I wasn't good enough, that my body wasn't good enough, that what I did wasn't good enough...every direction I looked, I felt I came up against that lie again and again.
Only to me it wasn't a lie, it was truth; I believed it 100%. I just wasn't enough.

I spiralled further and further into a pit of pain and negativity where I would wallow in my own self-doubt, allowing each negative experience to provide 'evidence' to prove that I am not enough. In a strange kind of way, I liked it there; it was a place where I was 'right', and it felt comfortable. Being in that negative cycle became a self-fulfilling prophecy. I would feel less than enough, so expect to be made to feel less than enough. This caused me to view life through a lens of rejection and 'being not good enough,' and then I would go on to have another experience of feeling less than enough, which set the cycle off again.

Is any of this sounding familiar?

I hit my 'Enough is Enough!' moment a few years ago, I was in the depths of depression, I couldn't find anything I liked about myself and I just knew I needed something to change. My husband was away, my children were playing up and life felt SO hard. I had a million excuses as to why sitting in my self-pity was justified, but one day I found the strength and had the clarity to stand up and say ENOUGH IS ENOUGH!! And yes, I did shout out loud! Ditching the lies is a choice, you need to actively choose God's truth above the lies that you are hearing, thinking and feeling.

Is it easy? Heck no! Is it worth it? YES!!

This Journal is in no way a quick fix to gain self-confidence or an answer to depression or anxiety but what I've come to realise is that God takes our 'Enough is Enough!' moments and transforms them into a beautiful journey of self-discovery and personal growth. It is a journey, not a destination, and one on which he promises to walk alongside us.

Choosing to ditch the lies is a step on that journey, a marker of a decision to choose Life.

For God has not given us a spirit of fear; but of power, and of love and of a sound mind.

1 Timothy 1:7

Ok, so what am I talking about when I say let's ditch the lies? A lie is a false statement, so when we choose to believe a lie and take it on as truth, it affects us. The world so often tells us that we are not good enough and parents, teachers, friends, partners, etc can also contribute to that feeling, whether knowingly or not.

Our hearts were created to connect with our father God's, to hear his truth and love for us and to give that back in response. They are made soft and open, ready to receive love, but we live in a fallen world, so as we have grown through the years our hearts have not always been treated with the respect and unconditional love that they were created for. We put walls up to protect our precious hearts and sometimes they get hardened through hurt. We are left feeling like something is missing, we are left not feeling enough.

These journal questions are here to encourage you to dig deep, helping you to find the areas where you are not feeling enough. They will enable you to recognise some of the roots, that can then be pulled out through forgiveness. I would recommend setting aside specific time to journal through these. Don't overthink what you are writing just allow it to flow and read it back afterwards. Sometimes we need God to highlight things for us and allow him to speak through our journalling. I encourage you to settle into a comfy spot, away from distractions and pray this prayer with me before you begin.

Holy Spirit, I invite you into this healing process. I give you permission to speak to and through me. Would you shown me any lies that I have believed about myself and highlight any roots of bitterness or unforgiveness that have made home in my heart. Please comfort me as I release the hurts I have been holding, into Jesus' hands and bring peace and wholeness to my heart again. Amen

What lies am I believing about myself and my circumstances?

I am not enough/I am always left out….

_____

_____

_____

_____

_____

_____

_____

_____

_____

_____

_____

_____

_____

_____

_____

In which areas do I lack confidence? Why?

I find it hard to stand in front of people. My teacher shouted at me in front of the class as a child and I've struggled since

_____

_____

_____

_____

_____

_____

_____

_____

_____

_____

_____

_____

_____

_____

_____

_____

Is there anybody that I need to forgive?

My friend hurt me when they said....

_____

_____

_____

_____

_____

_____

_____

_____

_____

_____

_____

_____

_____

_____

_____

_____

Have I made any judgements about myself or others?
These often start with I/They - always/never/can't etc

I will never be as good as ....../I always mess up

_____

_____

_____

_____

_____

_____

_____

_____

_____

_____

_____

_____

_____

_____

_____

_____

_____

_____

_____

_____

_____

_____

_____

_____

_____

_____

_____

_____

_____

_____

_____

Take some time to go back through the journalling you've done in this section. Highlight any lies that have come up and people who have contributed to those false beliefs about yourself that you need to forgive. There's space to make notes on the next page.

Notes

Forgiveness

Through my teenage years and early 20's I struggled massively with rejection. I often felt left out or overlooked and that pang of rejection and not being enough was a regular feeling. When we are viewing a situation through a lens, it can evoke many feelings that were never intended for us. We can attach hurt to people who have no idea they did anything wrong and we can exaggerate situations in our minds. I did this often and most of the time I didn't even recognise I was seeing things through this lens, I just felt everyone was against me. I was in a victim mentality.

I have experienced healing ministry sessions and have forgiven people that I felt hurt by, but that same feeling of rejection kept rearing its head. I hadn't dealt with the root of the issue, so although I cleared some of the surface stuff, I hadn't gone deep enough to pull out the root of where the feeling of rejection had started.
This finally came to a head one night when I was sat on the sofa crying out to God, because I'd had enough of feeling this way. He took me into a vision and here's a brief summary of what I experienced.

'I was stood behind a door that was covered in locks of different shapes and sizes, some were small bathroom locks that slide across and others were big heavy padlocks. I shouted out to God and said "I'm trapped, where are you? I can't get out". I noticed a light under the door and heard him say "Beki, I am right here, you're not alone. All you need to do is unlock the door and let me in." I desperately started unlocking the bolts one by one, some flicked open but others were much harder to pull across or open. The voice from the other side of the door encouraged me to keep going when I wanted to give up. I finally came to the last one. A huge, rusty, old padlock.
"I can't open it; I don't have the key," I shouted in despair and exhaustion. "God replied. "You have the key; you just need to go and find it."

For the first time I looked around me and I realised I was in a garden, there were raised beds in front of me, so I walked down the middle of them. Some of them were full of beautiful flowers but others looked like they had been abandoned and were dry with a couple of weeds poking through the soil. I felt drawn to the bed on the end to the left. It was one of the abandoned ones. I saw a shovel propped up next to the raised bed and started to dig.

"I can't find anything" I said, feeling defeated. "Keep digging" he replied "You buried it a long time ago" I finally felt something under the shovel and reached into the hole. As soon as I wrapped my fingers around the key a memory of my sister being born came to me; the feelings of rejection and the thoughts of not being good enough anymore. The tears flowed freely as I sat in the dirt. "Did you find it?" came a loving voice. I walked back to the door and started to put the key in the lock. It was stiff and hard to turn. I cried out again for help and God's voice came back as a constant encouragement that I could do this.
I managed to unlock it and lift the giant padlock off the door. As soon as I had, the door burst open and I instantly felt the huge arms of my heavenly father holding me so tight. I felt safe and loved. After we had embraced for a while, he stood back and asked if I wanted to give him the padlock, which I was still clinging to tightly. I looked at it and said "no, I can't" The back and forward conversation went on for a while, him encouraging me that he would protect me and me wanting to hand over the padlock but not being able to. It felt like part of me, I had had it for so long I couldn't imagine life without it. I had allowed it to be my security and my safety net.

Eventually he said,
"Do you trust me?"
"Yes"
"Do you believe I can keep you safe?"

"Yes"
"Are you prepared to put your faith in me over this padlock you have created?"
 Cue huge pause and lots of tears…….
"yes"

He then reached out his hand towards me and I used every ounce of strength I had left to give him the padlock. It is one of the hardest moments I have ever experienced. As soon as the lock touched his hand, it turned to dust and blew away! I instantly felt free. I was no longer carrying that huge weight and for the first time in years my mind felt clear. He then held me again and I felt a new energy in my body, a new strength and a great peace. We then walked together through the garden and he told me that I had created the raised beds and separated things into sections. His intention for the garden was always that it would flow freely. We talked about the buried key and as we walked, colour started to come back and flowers began to grow.'

When I came out of that vision I looked down and my t-shirt was soaked through with tears and 2 hours had passed. That moment changed my life, I have never been the same since and I am free from that lens of rejection. I felt it was important to share my story because we all put locks on the door to our hearts. We reason away situations instead of acknowledging the hurt. We try to protect ourselves, and I know that for some of you, reading this story will give you permission to open your door too. When pain runs deep, we need to trust who we are giving that pain to. We need to know that if we bring down our wall of protection, we will find that security in God instead. Believe me, I know how hard it is to admit that I didn't trust God as much as I thought I did, to question whether he knows and loves me more than I know and love myself. But what I experienced that day was wholeness, grace, love and a connection like no other. It was a piotal moment that I will never go

back from, a grounding of truth that I am accepted, not rejected.

"Forgiveness is the key that unlocks the door of resentment and the handcuffs of hatred. It is a power that breaks the chains of bitterness and the shackles of selfishness."

Corrie Ten Boom, Clippings from My Notebook

Before we go any further, let's check our hearts and choose to put our trust in God.

Father God, would you show me if I have put up any walls in my heart to protect myself or if I have closed off the door to my heart. I repent of not trusting you to love and protect me fully. I invite you to come into the garden of my heart and work with me there to pull out any roots of pain, judgement or bitterness. I choose to put my trust solely in you Lord. Amen.

Now we are going to start letting go of some of these painful moments that we have been carrying. Some things may be easier than others to let go of, so be kind to yourself through the process and take it at your own pace. Remember, you are not alone.

Use your notes from the Ditching the lies section and the situations that came up for you. Write them down on the next page with who hurt you or was involved and what they did. Don't forget to forgive yourself and God if applicable too. God is good all the time but sometimes we blame him for things in our heart and attach hurt, so we need to forgive and let go of those feelings.

Who do I need to forgive?

Alesha

_____

_____

_____

_____

_____

_____

_____

_____

_____

_____

_____

_____

_____

_____

_____

What did they do?

She didn't invite me to an event and that made me feel left out

_____

_____

_____

_____

_____

_____

_____

_____

_____

_____

_____

_____

_____

_____

_____

_____

Using this prayer go through each of the people in your list and forgive and release them for the way that they hurt you and made you feel.

Father God, I choose to forgive............For .... I no longer want to carry this pain in my heart, I release them into your hands and trust your will in this situation. I trust you to protect me as I hand the pain that I have been carrying over to you. I choose to cut all unhealthy ties with this person and bless them, in Jesus, name. Amen

Let's also break agreement with those lies that we've believed. Go back to the lies in your notes from your previous journalling and any that came up for you through the forgiving process and insert them into this prayer.

Father God, I break agreement with the lie that..............I will no longer hold this as a truth in my life or operate out of it. I choose instead to stand on the truth of who you say I am. Amen

Notes

Who am I?

Well done for letting go of all that baggage!! How are you feeling? You may feel free and lighter, but you may also feel a bit lost. When we have been carrying hurt for a long time, we can take it on as part of our identity, so when we no longer have that, we need to fill the gap with truth. This section is all about YOU! It's time to rediscover who you really are, what you are capable of and the truth of who God created you to be!

We may not have ever met in person or had the chance to connect yet, but I think you are pretty special. I know that you were thought about way before you were born. You were created with a purpose and given unique giftings. You were fearfully and wonderfully made, and even if I know nothing else about you, that makes you pretty special!

My whole life I have battled against the things that make me who I am. I have allowed comparison to steal my joy instead of finding joy in my own creations. I have rejected the parts of me that made me stand out and have withdrawn into my comfort zone too often. The more I lean into being 'ME', the more I feel enough, which is ironic after spending years walking away from 'ME' to feel enough!

We need to stop looking to others to fill us, affirm us and accept us. When we look to others for those things, we experience the lack, rejection and judgement. There is only one who will never let us down, one who knows us inside out and one who loves unconditionally. It's time to start putting God first and hearing his words above all others. As you answer these journal questions, listen to his words of truth over you, allow him to expose those things that you have hidden or pushed down and let him call them beautiful. As always, let it flow and as you read it back afterwards, let those words of truth sink into your heart and fill those places where you had been carrying a lie.

You are fearfully

and

wonderfully made

Psalm 139:14

Father God, Who do you say I am?

_____

_____

_____

_____

_____

_____

_____

_____

_____

_____

_____

_____

_____

_____

What talents and giftings have you placed inside of me? and why?

_____

_____

_____

_____

_____

_____

_____

_____

_____

_____

_____

_____

_____

_____

_____

_____

_____

What do you love about me?

_____

_____

_____

_____

_____

_____

_____

_____

_____

_____

_____

_____

_____

_____

_____

_____

What is my unique purpose? What are your plans for me?

_____

_____

_____

_____

_____

_____

_____

_____

_____

_____

_____

_____

_____

_____

_____

_____

_____

_____

_____

_____

_____

_____

_____

_____

_____

_____

_____

_____

_____

_____

Go back through your journalling in this section and highlight God's truths over your life and then write them onto the next page to create a list of truths that you can come back to again and again.

My Truths

Use this space to creatively document the truths that God has spoken over you through this process

Do you trust me?

Earlier in the journal I touched on trusting God and how we need to know in our hearts that he IS who he says he is. If we don't our relationship will only go so deep.

I have had a handful of times that God has said the words specifically – 'Do you trust me?' and it has felt like a pivotal moment, a choice as to whether I want to go deeper or not. He is kind and gracious and always gives us that choice. The story I shared earlier was one of those trust moments and one I said yes to. My yes was honoured in a big way and it was a transformational decision for me; yet I have also had times when I wasn't ready to say yes, I wasn't prepared to go that step deeper in my relationship. I don't believe in living in regret, but those are the moments that play on my mind from time to time, the 'what if?' moments. There is so much grace and love over those 'not yet' decisions, and the question will come back with another opportunity to choose trust. You have NOT missed out!

Growing up, Aladdin was one of my favourite films. My sister and I would fight over who got to be Jasmine and we'd watch the movie, reciting every line in character. Twice I have been given the same prophetic picture of the moment in Aladdin, where he is sat on the magic carpet and reaches his hand out to Jasmine as an invitation to join him and speaks the words, 'Do you trust me?' God wants to take us on an exciting adventure, full of wonder and delight but it can feel new and scary. He always gives us the choice to join him, he reaches out his hand with those same words 'Do you trust me?' We can choose to step out of our comfort zone, grab his hand and hold on, trusting he will protect us. Or we can stay in the safety of the walls of our castle. God now regularly uses that picture in my mind when I come up against decisions and maybe it will encourage you too.

God IS
who he
says he is

I encourage you to read the *Fathers Love Letter* by Barry Adams which you can find at *www.fathersloveletter.com* and these scriptures that highlight who God is.

There is also space to journal about the nature of God and record any other scriptures that come to you. Stand on that truth as you move forward.

Scriptures to meditate on God's nature

1 John 1:5 - God is light

Hebrews 13:8 - God is constant

Isaiah 40:28 – God is everlasting

Isaiah 41:10/matthew 28:20 – God is with you

Micah 7:18-19 – God is compassionate

1 corinthians 10:13 – God is faithful

Psalm 91:11 – God cares/protects

Ephesians 1:7 - God redeems

1 Peter 2:9 - God chose you

Psalm 103:13 - God is a father

Titus 3:4-7 - God is Kind

Father God, Who are you?

_____

_____

_____

_____

_____

_____

_____

_____

_____

_____

_____

_____

_____

_____

_____

_____

_____

_____

Are there any areas where I am trying to control rather than trust?

_____

_____

_____

_____

_____

_____

_____

_____

_____

_____

_____

_____

_____

_____

_____

_____

Father God, Can I trust you?

_____

_____

_____

_____

_____

_____

_____

_____

_____

_____

_____

_____

_____

_____

_____

_____

Standing

on truth

If you have worked through the journal with me, you will have ditched the lies, forgiven, discovered who you are and who God is. Now we are going to lay some foundations of truth that you can come back to and speak over yourself.

I shared about how I struggled with depression and hit a tough time while my husband was working away. During this time, I decided I needed to invest in myself, I had become bottom of the pile and I was struggling. I chose to invest time and money to give myself space to work through some of these things. I felt drawn to a lady who has a ministry coming alongside women. I connected with her instantly as we have a similar heart for women, and I felt safe with her to be open and vulnerable. I met with her once a month for 6 months and giving myself that time out to just be in God's presence and walk through some of the hard things was the BEST gift I could have ever given myself. I had never invested in myself financially like that before, but somewhere amid everything else I found my worth. I am worthy of love and acceptance, I am worthy of time out with God, I am worthy of being blessed. I came out of that time changed, and with a different mindset. I started my business Believe in ME because of that shift into believing truth over the lies. Four truths came out of one of my sessions – I am Worthy, I am Loved, I am Beautiful, and I am Enough. I wrote them on post it notes and stuck them on my mirror. I now have my affirmation cards which are much prettier, but there was something beautiful and raw about having those handwritten words in front of me each day, words that God had spoken straight to my heart. I speak those truths over myself daily.

This last section of the journal is about building on the truths you've already discovered. We have walked the journey from feeling 'Enough is Enough!' and now it's time to know that being Enough IS Enough. You don't have to be or do anything; you are enough just as you are. You are loved and accepted by your Father in heaven. That's the foundation that everything else is built on. Allow him to speak that truth over you and use this space to dig even deeper.

Father God, Am I enough just as I am?

_____

_____

_____

_____

_____

_____

_____

_____

_____

_____

_____

_____

_____

_____

_____

_____

_____

_____

You've worked through this journal and got to know yourself and God better along the way. You have processed hurts, lies and things that have held you back. Now it's time to write a statement of love and acceptance that you can speak over yourself, a beacon of truth in your day. If you struggle with this, go back to the 'My Truths' page and use the words God has spoken over you to create a power statement of truth!

Statement of love and acceptance

_____

_____

_____

_____

_____

_____

_____

_____

_____

_____

_____

_____

_____

_____

_____

_____

_____

How can I create a solid foundation of God's Truth in my life?
(Reading scripture, worship, journalling, declarations etc)

_____

_____

_____

_____

_____

_____

_____

_____

_____

_____

_____

_____

_____

_____

_____

_____

Choose 5 of your Truths here to speak over yourself daily to replace the lies you have broken agreement with. (Feel free to write them out and stick these up where you will see them too!)

1. _____

2. _____

3. _____

4. _____

5. _____

You started this journal feeling 'Enough is Enough!', you were fed up of being ruled by the hurts you'd experienced and making decisions from a place of fear.

Through the journey of this journal you have discovered some of the lies you've been carrying and have chosen to forgive the people who have hurt you. You've delved into discovering who you are and trusted God in the process. The truths you have uncovered in your journalling lay a foundation of God's love for you to stand on as you move forward.

This is an ongoing journey, a lifestyle of healing. Use the tools in this journal to deal with things as they come up. Keep your heart soft and your eyes fixed on Jesus.

Spare journalling pages for all of those extra bits that come up!

A Note from the author

Hello, I'm Beki!

An introverted, over-thinker who verbally processes but also likes to journal it out!
I am an avid fruit tea drinker and lover of all things blue. The beach is my happy place along with walks in the woods.

I am married to a wonderful man and have 4 children but get the honour of parenting 3 on this earth. My hope is that my girls grow up knowing that they belong. That they feel loved and accepted and pursue the fullness of God's glory over their lives.

This journal comes straight from my heart. A labour of love fuelled by a passion to see women walking in wholeness and embracing who God created them to be, not held back by fear, shame or self-doubt.

I founded my business Believe in ME to come alongside women on their journey. To help them go from fear, shame and self-doubt to freedom and confidence in themselves by having encounters with God and going deeper in their relationship with him.

I am all about connection. It's a foundational value for me. If you also enjoy genuine and authentic interactions come and chat over on the socials or get in touch via the website.

@believeinmeaffirmations
www.believeinmeaffirmations.co.uk

Dear Heart Letters Series

At the end of 2019 I launched a new blog series called Dear Heart Letters. I wanted to create a platform for women to share their heart and voice, a space to be vulnerable and allow others to do the same.
It is a collection of letters from women to their hearts. A series of raw honesty and beautiful healing that invites others to embrace their own life experiences.
Here I share the first letter in the series.

If you would like to get involved and collaborate on this blog series by sharing your own Dear Heart Letter.
Please get in touch on social media or by emailing hello@believeinmeaffirmations.co.uk

Dear Heart,

It's been a while since we really talked. I'm sorry I've not shown you the love and affection you deserve.

You have been through so much over the years. You have been beaten and bruised by others and by me. I should have been kinder, I'm sorry for taking my hurt and frustration out on you.

You are strong. You have given pieces of yourself to others so selflessly and sometimes they have not been treasured the way that they should. That must have really hurt you, but you carry on. You keep trying.

I know you felt broken when you walked through the grief of baby loss, you felt torn and raw, you longed to stay connected. I think you are so brave, and I love that you have a special place to hold all the memories of those dearest to you.

I'm sorry for the times that I've shut you in and tried to protect you. I thought I was doing the right thing, but I see now that you need to feel, even when it hurts. It's who you are. I promise not to shut you down again.

You are free to be you, to create and to just be. I love you heart, just as you are. Beautifully you. You bear scars of your past, but they make you interesting and unique. You beat with a rhythm that is in time with your maker. The love you pour out into me is so rich and sweet.

I love that we can work together instead of against each other. We have come so far and I wouldn't want to do this without you.

Thinking of you,
Mind x

Printed in Poland
by Amazon Fulfillment
Poland Sp. z o.o., Wrocław